HANDS-ON
Science

Matter and Materials

Peter Mellett

Illustrated by David Le Jars

KING*f*ISHER

NEW YORK

KINGFISHER
Larousse Kingfisher Chambers Inc.
95 Madison Avenue
New York, New York 10016
www.kingfisherpub.com

Produced for Kingfisher by PAGE*One*

First published in 2001
10 9 8 7 6 5 4 3 2 1

1TR/1200/TWP/GRST/150SMA

LIBRARY OF CONGRESS CATALOGING-IN-PUBLICATION DATA
has been applied for.

ISBN 0-7534-5350-9

Printed in Singapore

For PAGE*One*
Creative Director Bob Gordon
Project Editor Miriam Richardson
Designers Monica Bratt, Tim Stansfield

For Kingfisher
Managing Editor Clive Wilson
Coordinating Editor Laura Marshall
Production Manager Oonagh Phelan
DTP Coordinator Nicky Studdart

CONTENTS

Getting started

The world we live in is made from matter. Matter includes anything that has mass and takes up space. Our bodies, the air we breathe, and the water we drink are all examples of matter. The different types of matter we use to make things are called materials.

Some materials, like rocks, soil, air, water, and wood, are natural.

Other materials, like glass, plastic, and paper, are made by people, or manufactured.

This book shows you how different kinds of matter and materials behave. It will help you understand how different materials are tested and chosen before they are used in manufacturing or building.

The right stuff

You'll need a few everyday things, like string, rubber bands, plastic bottles, and some other items you can find in the kitchen.

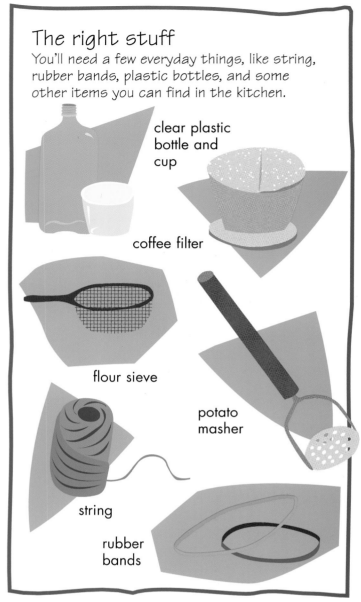

clear plastic bottle and cup

coffee filter

flour sieve

potato masher

string

rubber bands

Getting organized

Carry out your experiments on a sturdy table. But don't forget to cover it with newspaper first, to protect its surface.

If you need to pour water, put a shallow pan underneath to catch any spills.

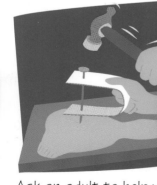

Ask an adult to help you use a hammer. Hammer on a firm surface, like the floor, and use scrap wood to protect it.

Clock symbol

The clock symbol at the beginning of each experiment shows you how many minutes the activity should take. All of the experiments take between 5 and 40 minutes. If you are using glue, allow extra time for drying.

Warning

Some activities involve heat, flames, or the use of a hammer. Ask an adult for help with these and with any other activities where you see this warning symbol.

Don't touch your face or rub your eyes, especially if you are using materials such as salt, baking soda, or soil.

Always wash your hands and scrub your nails thoroughly after you have finished working.

Having problems?

Don't give up if you have problems with some of the activities at first. Even Einstein had his bad days!

If things don't seem to be working, reread each step of the activity and try again.

If you get really stuck, remember that adults at home can help you with explanations. Your teachers can help too.

Stuck for words?

If you come across a word you don't understand or if you just want to find out more, take a look at the glossary on pages 38 and 39.

Denting and squeezing

Different materials have different properties. For example, the materials your clothes are made of are soft and stretchy, but materials used for building, such as concrete and brick, are hard and strong. Scientists test materials to measure and compare their properties. Then they can choose the best materials for making or manufacturing different things.

Hard or soft?

Trying to dent or scratch a material helps show how hard it is. Ask an adult to help you with this activity.

YOU WILL NEED
- A 4-IN. (10-CM) NAIL
- A HAMMER
- AN OLD SOCK
- A PIECE OF CARDBOARD 2 IN. (5CM) BY 9¾ IN. (25CM)
- A MAGNIFYING GLASS
- A PIECE OF SCRAP WOOD
- SOME SOLID MATERIALS, LIKE WOOD, A CLAY POT, PLASTIC AND METAL SPOONS, A STONE, AND AN ERASER

20

1 Make a hole ¾ in. (2cm) from each end of the cardboard strip. Bend the strip into a "U" shape and push the nail through the holes, making sure it is held firmly.

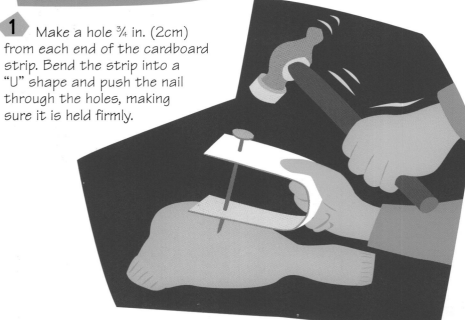

2 Put one of your solid materials inside the sock on top of the scrap wood. Place the nail's point on top of the solid. Hit the head of the nail firmly—the hammer should drop no more than 6 in. (15cm).

3 Take the solid out of the sock. Use the magnifying glass to see whether the nail has dented or scratched the material. Now try doing steps 2 and 3 with the other materials and see what happens to them.

What's happening?

Different materials react in different ways to being hit hard. Some, like stone and pottery, are so hard they can't be dented at all. But they are brittle and sometimes shatter. Others, like metals, are hard, but not brittle. The nail will leave a small scratch on them. Materials like wood are softer, and the nail will make a hole in them. Plastics can be soft, hard, durable, or brittle.

Squeezing materials

Place your samples on the newspaper and squeeze them, one at a time, under the potato masher. What happens to each material as you steadily increase the force?

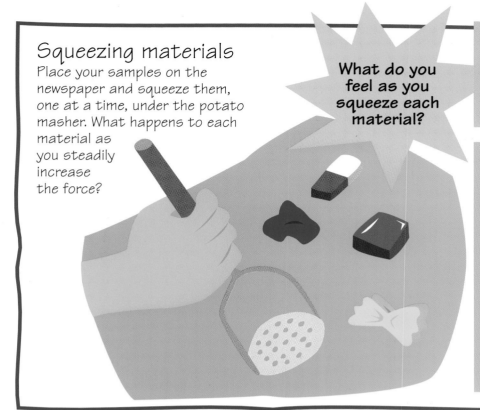

What do you feel as you squeeze each material?

YOU WILL NEED
◆ A POTATO MASHER
◆ SMALL PIECES OF AN ERASER, DRIED PASTA, AND MODELING CLAY
◆ A PIECE OF NEWSPAPER

5

What's happening?

Squeezing a material tests how well it stands up to a force called compression. Elastic materials, like the eraser, spring back when the force stops. Brittle substances, like dried pasta, shatter instead. Modeling clay isn't elastic like the eraser. The force breaks it up so it is squeezed through the holes of the potato masher.

FLASHBACK

The first metal

About 6,500 years ago, people in Egypt were the first to discover metal, in the form of copper. Like most metals, copper is found in stony materials called ore. The Egyptians put the ore into a furnace, then blasted air into it to make the charcoal burn white hot. This freed the copper so they could collect it and use it to make things.

MATERIALS ALL AROUND YOU

How much of our world today is natural? The natural materials you are most likely to see are wood, stone, cotton, and wool. Metals like iron, steel, copper, and aluminum come from rocky ore. Most materials are manufactured. Plastics are made from crude oil.

Stretching and snapping

The extent to which a material can be pulled and stretched is called its tensile strength. Materials with a high tensile strength are chosen by engineers to do certain jobs. The steel cable of a crane, for example, has a high tensile strength and is able to support a very heavy load.

Threads and wires

Compare the tensile strength of three different materials. Remember to use a different thread each time!

YOU WILL NEED
- A 2-LITER PLASTIC BOTTLE
- A BROOM
- TWO STOOLS OR CHAIRS
- A MEASURING CUP
- WATER
- A MARKER
- THREE THREADS OF THE SAME THICKNESS, LIKE WOOL YARN, NYLON DENTAL FLOSS, AND COPPER FUSE WIRE

20

1 Lay the broom flat on top of the two stools, as shown in the picture.

2 Measure 4 oz. (120ml) of water and pour it into the bottle. Mark the level of the water and label it "4 oz." Repeat this step, labeling the marks "8 oz.," "12 oz.," and so on up to 36 oz.

3 Pour the water out. Tie the end of one thread around the neck of the bottle and the other end around the broom handle. The bottle should hang a little above the floor.

4 Support the bottle with one hand and slowly pour water in. After every 4 oz. (120ml), replace the cap, then let go of the bottle. When the thread breaks, note the water level in the bottle. Repeat steps 3 and 4 with the other threads. Which one lasts the longest?

What's happening?
Gravity pulls down on the water in the bottle. This creates a pulling force, called tension, in the thread, which causes it to stretch and then snap. How quickly the thread snaps depends on how thick it is and what it is made from. Wool, a natural fiber, isn't very strong. Dental floss, made from a type of plastic called nylon, and copper fuse wire both have much higher tensile strength than wool.

Testing sheets

Cut a strip from each material, ⅓ in. (1cm) by 6 in. (15cm). Wrap a strip tightly around the clothespin and hold it firmly. Squeeze the clothespin harder and harder until the material breaks. Do this with each strip.

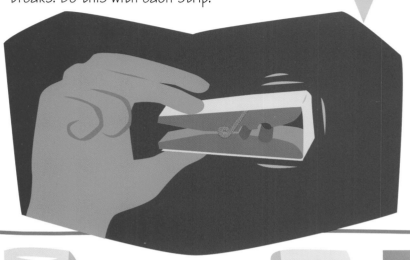

Which materials snap most easily?

What's happening?

Some materials are more elastic than others, which means they stretch further before they break. Plastic materials like plastic wrap are made from particles called molecules. These hold together strongly, stretching before they break apart. But paper materials are made from fibers, which break easily.

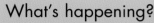

FLASHBACK

Plastic bags

Polyethylene, one of the most common plastic materials, was invented in 1933. It is made from a gas called ethylene. It was first used to insulate cables in aircraft radar sets. In the 1950s, polyethylene replaced paper for wrapping food. Nowadays, you may carry your groceries in a polyethylene bag.

STRONG STEEL
A crane's cables are made from steel. The tensile strength of steel is four times greater than copper and ten times greater than nylon. Steel cables can support huge loads without breaking.

Soil

Soil is one of the most important materials in the world. Almost all plants need soil to grow, and most animals depend on plants for food. Without soil, there would be almost no life on land. There are many different kinds of soil, but all of them are a mixture of sand, clay, and the rotted remains of dead plants, called humus.

Testing soil

Find out what your local soil is like. How much water does it absorb, and how well does water drain through it?

> ### YOU WILL NEED
> ◆ DRY SOIL **20**
> ◆ A 15-OZ. (500-ML) PLASTIC BOTTLE
> ◆ A SPOON
> ◆ SCISSORS
> ◆ COTTON WOOL
> ◆ A TABLESPOON
> ◆ A MEASURING CUP
> ◆ WATER

1 Cut the bottle in half. Make two cuts down each side of the lower part of the bottle. Fold the cut parts inward to make four tabs.

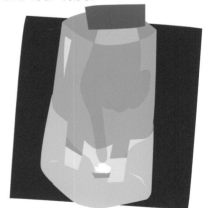

2 Turn the top half of the bottle upside down to make a funnel. Now push it into the bottom half of the bottle so that the tabs grip the bottle neck. Push a ball of cotton wool into the bottle neck.

3 Add six tablespoons of soil and then gently pour in 6 oz. (200ml) of water. Time how long it takes the water to pass through the soil. Then measure the amount of water that runs out of the soil.

What's happening?

Water drains through soil by trickling through the spaces between the soil particles. Not all of the added water drains out, because some is absorbed by the clay and humus in the soil. The sandier the soil, the more water will drain out. This is because sand does not absorb water. Clay particles are hundreds of times smaller than sand grains. They block the spaces between sand and humus and slow the downward movement of water. Water cannot pass at all through some clay soils. You can tell from the amount of water that drains through whether your soil is made of sand or clay.

What's in your soil?

Fill one fourth of the bottle with soil, then fill two thirds with water. Screw on the cap and shake hard. Let the bottle stand. Can you see the different layers forming as the soil settles?

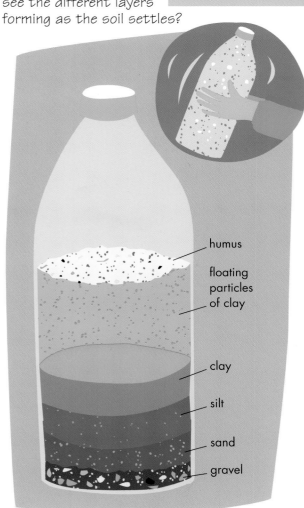

- humus
- floating particles of clay
- clay
- silt
- sand
- gravel

What's happening?

Large grains of sand and gravel are the first to settle to the bottom. The next layer up is fine, silty sand, followed by clay particles. Floating above the clay layer are tiny clay particles too small to settle to the bottom. You may also see humus floating on the surface. By testing different soil samples, you can see how soil varies from place to place.

Hard rock

Rub each rock sample on the sandpaper to see how easily it crumbles into powder. Then look at each rock's surface to see how smooth or rough it is.

Which rocks crumble most easily?

What's happening?

Sandpaper is coated with very hard and rough, or abrasive, particles. They cut easily into soft rock and break it down into a sandy powder. The weather has the same effect on rocks, but it takes millions of years to change large boulders into grains of sand.

SCARCE SOIL
Soil contains chemicals that all plants need to grow. Even where soil is scarce, like on a mountainside, tiny pockets of soil can sustain some hardy plants.

Moving heat

Heat moves through solids by a process called conduction. Some materials, like metals, allow heat to pass easily. They are good conductors of heat. Other materials, like paper and plastics, do not allow heat to pass easily. They are called insulators and are poor conductors of heat. We use insulating materials to keep things warm.

Heat loss
Hot drinks cool down because heat moves from the hot liquid to the cooler air outside.

Keeping warm

Find out which insulating material keeps a hot drink hottest for longest.

YOU WILL NEED
20
- FOUR CERAMIC MUGS
- A LARGE PLASTIC BAG
- FOUR THIN RUBBER BANDS
- NEWSPAPER
- COTTON WOOL
- HOT (NOT BOILING) WATER
- A CLOCK

1 Wrap layers of newspaper around a mug and hold them in place with a rubber band. Cover another mug with cotton wool. Place the third mug upright in an open plastic bag. Leave the fourth uncovered.

2 Ask an adult to heat some water until it is hot, but not boiling. Fill each mug to the same level, ¾ in. (2cm) from the top. Tightly seal the plastic bag with a rubber band so it fits loosely around the mug.

What's happening?
The mug in the plastic bag will probably be the hottest, while the uncovered mug is the coolest. Air is a good insulator, but the open air around the uncovered mug moves around too much to insulate well. The plastic bag holds a layer of air around the hot mug—this stops heat from escaping. Cotton wool has air trapped between its fluffy fibers. Newspaper also contains air, but less than cotton wool. Most insulating materials use trapped air to keep heat from flowing away.

3 After 15 minutes, use a finger to test the water in each mug. Arrange the four mugs in order, from the hottest to the coolest.

Testing heat conduction

Stick a bead to the handle end of each spoon with a blob of butter or margarine. Stand the bowl on the newspaper and arrange the spoons so their handles stick out around the rim. Ask an adult to pour freshly boiled water into the bowl. How long does it take for the beads to drop from each spoon?

YOU WILL NEED
- BUTTER OR MARGARINE **20**
- METAL, PLASTIC, AND WOODEN SPOONS
- A HEATPROOF GLASS BOWL
- THREE SMALL PLASTIC BEADS
- BOILED WATER (ASK AN ADULT)
- NEWSPAPER

What makes the beads drop off?

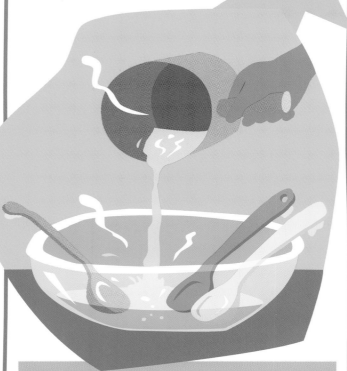

What's happening?

Conduction carries heat up the handle of each spoon, which causes the butter to melt and the bead to fall off. Metal is a better conductor than wood or plastic. The end of the metal spoon becomes hot most quickly, so the bead drops off from this spoon first. It takes the most time for the bead to fall from the wooden spoon because wood contains air and is a poor conductor of heat.

Heat energy

Two hundred years ago, scientists thought that heat was an invisible fluid. But in 1851, William Thomson introduced the modern idea that heating something increases the energy of its particles and makes them move around more rapidly.

WINTER WARMTH
Have you ever wondered why birds puff themselves up in cold weather? Under their feathers are fluffy fibers that trap layers of air. These insulating layers reduce heat loss and keep the birds warm.

Solids, liquids, and gases

Our world is made from millions of different materials, but all this matter exists in just three forms—solids, liquids, and gases. Solids, like bricks and ice cubes, are hard and have a fixed shape. Liquids, like water, are runny and do not have a fixed shape. They fill the bottom of a container and make a flat surface. Gases, like air, spread out in all directions, so they are often kept in closed containers.

Feel the difference

See what happens when you try to squeeze a gas (air), a liquid (water), and a solid (ice). You'll need extra time to make the ice in step 3.

YOU WILL NEED
- A 15-OZ. (500-ML) PLASTIC BOTTLE WITH A SCREW CAP
- WATER
- A LONG BALLOON
- A FREEZER

15

1 Screw the cap tightly on the empty bottle and squeeze it in your hand. What happens to the bottle?

2 Now unscrew the cap and fill the bottle with water until it overflows. Screw the cap on tightly and try squeezing the bottle again. Can you squeeze it easily?

3 Fill a balloon with water and tie the end. Squeeze the balloon and feel how the water moves around inside. Then place the balloon in the freezer for several hours. Can you move the water around inside the balloon?

What's happening?

Air, a gas, is compressible, which means it can be squeezed into a smaller space. Water, a liquid, is not compressible, which is why you can't squeeze the bottle filled with water. Liquids and gases are called fluids because they can flow from one place to another. When the temperature falls below 32°F (0°C), water freezes to make solid ice. Solids cannot flow, and they are not compressible.

Gases have mass

Tie a piece of string to each end of the wooden rod. Tie the other end of each string to the tab on a can. Hang the rod by its center underneath the stool so that the cans are evenly balanced. Ask an adult to gently pull the tab on one can to open it slightly, just until you hear a small "whoosh" sound. Then let the cans hang in balance.

How does the balance change over the next half hour?

What's happening?

You'll see that the balance of the cans is disturbed and that the open can rises slightly. This is because soft drinks contain a gas called carbon dioxide dissolved in flavored water. Once the can has been opened, the carbon dioxide slowly escapes from the liquid, causing the mass of the liquid to decrease. This means the contents of the open can weigh less than they did when it was closed.

FLASHBACK

John Dalton was an English chemist who lived from 1766 to 1844. He said that matter is made up of invisible particles. In solid materials the particles are fixed together, but in liquids they can slide around past each other. The particles in gases are far apart and travel at great speed.

UNDER PRESSURE

Gases, like air, are made up of particles that are far apart. But to inflate this rescue dinghy, air has been pumped in under pressure, which squeezes the air particles closely together. The air makes the dinghy firm and buoyant in the water.

Mixing materials

Most materials are not made of a single, pure substance. They are usually made up of different substances mixed together in different ways. For example, pastry dough is a mixture of flour, fat, and water, while soft drinks consist of water, sugar, flavorings, and carbon dioxide gas. The right ingredients must be chosen to make up each mixture.

Solutions

You can mix water with sugar or salt to make a mixture called a solution. The solution behaves differently to ordinary water.

YOU WILL NEED
- WARM WATER **20**
- SOLID, GRANULATED MATERIALS, LIKE SUGAR, SALT, AND SAND
- FOUR CLEAR PLASTIC CUPS
- A TEASPOON
- A MAGNIFYING GLASS
- A FREEZER

Which of the grains disappear in the water?

1 Sprinkle a few grains of each solid on the table. Look at them through the magnifying glass. Can you see a difference in their shape and size? The grains of salt and sugar have straight sides—they are called crystals.

2 Fill one of the cups halfway with warm water. Add a pinch of sugar and watch what happens to each grain. Then add a heaped spoonful of sugar and stir the mixture. What happens to the grains now?

3 Fill another cup halfway with water. Put this and the cup of sugary water in the freezer for two or three hours. Check them every 15 minutes to see what's happening. Now repeat steps 2 and 3 with the salt, then the sand.

What's happening?

Sugar and salt crystals break down, or dissolve, when they are mixed with water. We call the result a sugar solution or a salt solution. When the crystals dissolve, they break into particles that are too small to see. These particles spread evenly through the water. The dissolved substance makes the solution freeze at a lower temperature than a pure liquid would, so the sugar and salt solutions will take longer to freeze than the pure water. Unlike sugar and salt, sand is insoluble—it doesn't dissolve.

Mix it up

Ask an adult to help you collect all the ingredients and equipment needed to bake a cake. Watch how the ingredients change as you mix them together. Then see the mixture change again as it bakes in the oven.

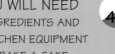

How do you change soggy cake batter into a cake?

What's happening?

A baked cake looks and tastes very different from the original raw ingredients. Cake batter usually contains flour, eggs, sugar, and fat. While it cooks in the oven, heat makes the mixture expand and changes its color, texture, and taste.

FLASHBACK

Going for gold

Alchemists were early chemists who worked more than 400 years ago. They boiled, melted, and dissolved things, like chemists do today. Alchemists believed that if they mixed the right ingredients together, they could change cheap metals into gold. They didn't understand that elements (like gold) only occur naturally and cannot be made by mixing other substances.

WOOD YOU BELIEVE IT?

Wood is a very useful natural material, but one problem is that a plank of wood can only be as wide as a tree trunk. Chipboard is made from wood chippings and sawdust bonded together by resin glue. It is made into sheets up to six feet (2m) wide, then cut to the shape and size needed.

Expanding and contracting

When heat is applied to a solid, liquid, or gas, the heat energy causes the substance to take up more space, or expand. When the substance is cooled, it loses energy and takes up less space, or contracts. Water is an exception to this rule: frozen water takes up more space than the same amount of water in liquid form.

Hot and cold air

Air is an invisible gas. This activity helps you see how air expands and contracts when it is heated and cooled. Be careful with glass and hot water—ask an adult for help.

YOU WILL NEED   15
- A SMALL, STRONG GLASS BOTTLE, SUCH AS AN EMPTY KETCHUP BOTTLE
- A DRINKING STRAW
- MODELING CLAY
- A DISH TOWEL
- A BOWL OF HOT WATER (ASK AN ADULT)
- A COLD, WET DISH TOWEL

What's happening?
The bottle is full of air. Heating the bottle heats up the air inside. Heat energy makes the tiny particles of air move around faster, so they take up more space. This makes the air expand, and it bubbles out of the straw. But cooling the bottle makes the air particles slow down and take up less space. The air contracts, and water is pulled into the empty space in the bottle.

1 Gently wrap a ball of modeling clay around the straw near one end, leaving the end open. Push the clay into the neck of the bottle to make an airtight seal.

2 Ask an adult to soak the dish towel in the bowl of hot water and wrap it around the bottle.

3 Turn the wrapped bottle upside down and dip the end of the straw into the bowl of water. What do you see?

4 Keep the end of the straw below the surface of the water. Unwrap the hot towel, then wrap the cold towel around the bottle. Watch what happens to the water!

In hot water

Use the same equipment as before. This time, fill the bottle to the top with cold water before you attach the straw. Some water should rise about halfway up the straw; use a pencil to mark how high it rises. Now stand the bottle in a bowl of hot water and watch the water level in the straw.

YOU WILL NEED
10
- BOTTLE, STRAW, AND MODELING CLAY, AS BEFORE
- A BOWL OF HOT WATER (ASK AN ADULT)
- A PENCIL

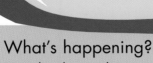

Does the water expand as much as the air did?

What's happening?
Particles that make up a liquid (water) move more slowly than particles in a gas (air). They are closer together and slide past each other as they move. Heating a liquid makes the particles move faster, so the liquid expands. But they do not move as fast as gas particles do, so liquid does not expand as much as gas does.

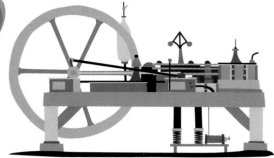

Lenoir engine

First built in 1860, Lenoir engines were the forerunners of modern gasoline and diesel engines. All these "internal combustion" engines burn a mixture of fuel and air inside a cylinder. The heat makes the gases expand, which forces a piston to move inside the cylinder. The piston is attached to a crank that works like the pedals of a bicycle to turn a wheel.

HOT STUFF
The hollow bulb at the end of a thermometer contains a liquid metal called mercury. As the temperature increases, the mercury expands. It moves through a thin tube inside the thermometer, which is marked to show the temperature.

Heating substances

When you heat a substance, its temperature increases. This rise in temperature changes the appearance of many substances. For example, water bubbles when it boils, and bread changes into toast. When heating stops, the temperature falls again. Water stops bubbling, so we say that the change is only temporary. Toast, on the other hand, does not change back into bread when it cools. The heat has caused a permanent change.

Gentle heating

Some substances change when the temperature rises only slightly. When you do this activity, don't touch the lamp bulb—it will get hot.

YOU WILL NEED
◆ A PAT OF BUTTER
◆ A PIECE OF CHOCOLATE
◆ A PIECE OF CANDLE WAX
◆ SUGAR
◆ ALUMINUM FOIL
◆ SCISSORS
◆ AN ADJUSTABLE DESK LAMP
◆ A DRINKING STRAW

20

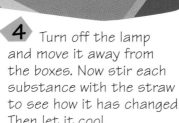

1 Cut four 4-in. (10-cm) squares from the aluminum foil. Fold up the edges and pinch the corners to make four small boxes with open tops and flat bottoms.

3 Ask an adult to turn on the lamp and point it straight down, about 2 in. (5cm) above the boxes. Watch for five minutes to see how heat from the lamp affects the different substances.

4 Turn off the lamp and move it away from the boxes. Now stir each substance with the straw to see how it has changed. Then let it cool.

2 Put a small amount of each substance into an aluminum box so that each box contains something different.

What's happening?
The lamp raises the temperature to about 165°F (74°C) and gently heats the four substances. The butter, chocolate, and candle wax all become liquids when they are heated this way. We say that they have melted. When they cool down again, they change back into solids—so melting is a temporary change. Sugar is not affected by the heat from an electric lamp and does not change at all.

Stronger heating

Some substances need stronger heat to make them change. Heat the oven to 400°F (200°C). Put a little sugar, salt, and egg into the aluminum boxes and place them on a cookie sheet. Ask an adult to put them in the oven and to take them out after 15 minutes. Which substances look different?

What's happening?

Sugar melts at this higher temperature to become a brown, sticky substance called caramel. This is a permanent change. When caramel cools, it becomes solid. Eggs bake in an oven. This change is also permanent, because particles in the sugar break apart and join up in a new way. Salt is not affected. It must be heated to over 1,560°F (849°C) before it melts. When cool, it becomes solid salt again.

High-temperature heating

Place some sugar on an old teaspoon. Ask an adult to light the tea light and hold the spoon over it for a while to heat it. What do you see?

What happens to the sugar?

What's happening?

Sugar is made from carbon, hydrogen, and oxygen. When heated to about 925°F (496°C), it breaks down into black carbon, which you see on the spoon, and steam, which rises. When this happens, we say the sugar decomposes. It is a permanant change.

BLOWING BUBBLES
Glass gradually gets softer as the temperature rises. To shape glass, workers blow down an iron pipe to make bubbles of glass expand. They cut open the bubbles to produce beautiful jugs and ornaments.

Changing state

Matter can exist in three states—as solids, liquids, or gases. When a substance is heated, it may change its state. Heat can make a solid melt to form a liquid or make a liquid boil to form a gas. These changes of state are temporary. Cooling reverses the changes—gases condense into liquids, and liquids freeze and become solid again.

From gas

to liquid

to solid

The air is full of invisible water vapor. You can use a freezing mixture to trap this gas and turn it into ice, which you can see.

YOU WILL NEED 30
- ◆ ICE
- ◆ A DISH TOWEL
- ◆ TWO RUBBER BANDS
- ◆ A ROLLING PIN
- ◆ SALT
- ◆ A LARGE, DARK-COLORED MUG
- ◆ A SPOON

FLASHBACK

See you later, water vapor

Over millions of years, flowing water has helped to shape the surface of the earth. Heat from the sun makes seawater change into water vapor, or evaporate. Vapor rises into the air, cools, and forms clouds of tiny water droplets. These droplets fall as rain. As rivers carry water back to the sea, they slowly carve out valleys between hills and mountains.

3 You will see that a white solid forms on the outside of the mug. It reaches up to the same level on the outside as the ice and salt inside. Scrape some of the solid into the spoon and watch it melt to form a liquid.

1 Line up ten ice cubes along one edge of the dish towel and roll it into a sausage shape. Twist a rubber band around each end of the towel and place it on a firm surface. Now crush the ice with the rolling pin.

2 Fill the mug halfway with crushed ice. Add about one fourth of a mugful of salt. Stir the mixture and then leave the mug undisturbed for about 20 minutes.

Boiling and evaporation

Wet two cotton handkerchiefs and wring them out. Hang one in a warm or sunny place and the other in a cool place. Check every five minutes to see how each one is drying.

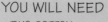
20

YOU WILL NEED
- TWO COTTON HANDKERCHIEFS
- A SUNNY SPOT OR A WARM PLACE INDOORS
- A COOL PLACE
- WATER

Which handkerchief dries faster?

What's happening?

You probably won't be surprised to see that the handkerchief in the warm place dries faster than the one in the cool place. But why is this? As water takes in heat from the surrounding air, it changes and becomes a gas called water vapor. When this happens, we say that the water has evaporated. The higher the temperature, the quicker the rate of evaporation. So the handkerchief in the warm place dries faster than the one in the cool place because the water evaporates from it more quickly.

What's happening?

The temperature of ice drops even lower when salt is added. The mixture inside the mug makes the outside extremely cold. The air around us is a gas that has water vapor dissolved in it. When this invisible vapor touches the outside of the mug, it condenses, which means it changes into liquid water. This immediately freezes into solid ice. When you scrape some of this into the spoon, it warms up and melts to form liquid water.

LIQUID STEEL
Steel melts at around 2,800°F (1,538°C). It glows white hot and is nearly eight times heavier than the same amount of water. Here liquid steel is being poured into molds to make parts for engines.

Permanent changes

As we have seen, some changes are temporary and can be reversed easily. For example, chocolate melts when it is heated, but changes back to solid chocolate when cooled. Other changes are permanent and cannot be reversed. For example, boiling an egg changes it permanently. There are three main ways of making permanent changes happen—by mixing substances together, by heating them, or by passing electricity through them.

Mix a change

Mixing vinegar and baking soda together creates carbon dioxide gas, which puts out flames. You must ask an adult to do steps 2 and 3 of this activity.

YOU WILL NEED
- BAKING SODA
- A HEATPROOF BOWL
- A SHORT CANDLE
- VINEGAR
- MODELING CLAY
- A DESSERTSPOON

15

1 Use the modeling clay to attach the candle firmly to the center of the bowl. Sprinkle five level spoonfuls of baking soda around the candle.

2 Ask an adult to light the candle, then to spoon vinegar down the inner side of the bowl, avoiding the flame. Watch how the liquid and powder froth as they mix.

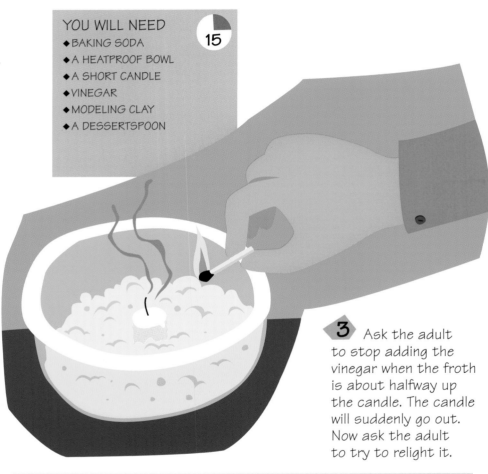

3 Ask the adult to stop adding the vinegar when the froth is about halfway up the candle. The candle will suddenly go out. Now ask the adult to try to relight it.

What's happening?

A permanent change takes place when baking soda and vinegar are mixed together. The particles in these two substances join up in a different way to make new substances. One of the new substances is a gas called carbon dioxide. It causes the mixture to froth. Carbon dioxide gas is heavier than air. Although you can't see it, it fills the bowl and puts out, or extinguishes, the flame. Carbon dioxide is used in many types of fire extinguishers.

Bake a model

Mold some bakeable modeling clay into a shape to make a model. Think about how it looks and feels while you do this. Then ask an adult to follow the instructions and bake your model in the oven. Let it cool. How does it look and feel now?

What changes happen when you bake the clay?

What's happening?

Modeling clay is soft and easy to squeeze. It is made of long, thin particles that slide past each other when you squeeze the clay. But once the clay has been baked in the oven, permanent links form between the particles. They can no longer slide around, which is why your baked model is now hard.

Electric effect

Ask an adult to strip the ends of the wires. Then ask them to connect one end of each wire to the battery and dip the other end into some salty water. What happens to the wires? Do you recognize the smell?

What's happening?

Electricity changes part of the salt solution into a gas, which makes bubbles. This gas is called chlorine. You often smell it at swimming pools, where it is used to disinfect the water.

CHEMICAL REACTION

These children are studying chemical reactions that make materials change permanently. The substances they start with are called reactants. After reactants change, they make new substances called products.

Burning

The scientific name for burning is combustion. When a fuel burns, it mixes with oxygen from the air, and a permanent change occurs that gives off heat. Solid fuels include wood and coal; gasoline and kerosene are liquid fuels. Before they can burn quickly, solid and liquid fuels must change into gases. Many common fuels produce carbon dioxide gas and water vapor when they burn.

! Air and fire

You can see how flames need oxygen to burn. You must ask an adult to do this activity while you watch.

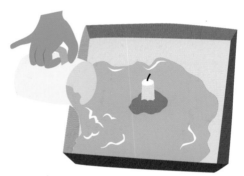

1 Use modeling clay to hold the candle upright in the middle of the pan. Pour water into the pan until it is about 3/4 in. (2cm) deep.

2 Ask an adult to light the candle and place the glass jar over it. The rim of the jar must be under the water, resting on the bottom of the pan.

YOU WILL NEED
20
◆ A CANDLE, ABOUT 2 IN. (5CM) TALL
◆ A METAL CAKE PAN
◆ A TALL GLASS JAR
◆ WATER
◆ MODELING CLAY

3 Watch the candle flame carefully as soon as the jar is in place. What happens to the level of the water inside the jar?

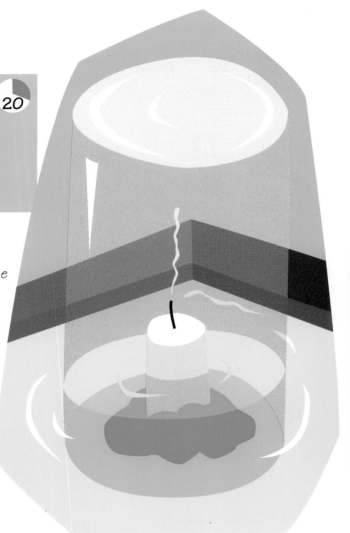

What's happening?
Fire needs oxygen to burn, but only about one fifth of air is oxygen. The rest is mostly a gas called nitrogen. When all the oxygen inside the jar is used, the flame goes out. Water rises into the jar to take the place of the oxygen that was used up by the burning.

Drilling for oil

Cars, trucks, ships, and planes use liquid fuels made from petroleum, which is also called crude oil. This dark, oily liquid comes from deep under the ground. The first oil well was drilled by Edwin L. Drake in 1859 at Titusville, Pennsylvania. He struck oil at a depth of just 75 feet (23m). Modern oil wells are up to 16,400 feet (5,000m) deep.

FIGHTING FIRE WITH FOAM
Firefighters spray foam onto burning aircraft fuel. Bubbles in the foam contain carbon dioxide gas and other chemicals that stop oxygen from helping the fuel burn. The foam smothers the fire and cools the burning fuel.

Take a closer look

Ask an adult to light the candle again. Look carefully—but not too closely—to see the three parts of the flame.

YOU WILL NEED
◆ A CANDLE, ABOUT 2 IN. (5CM) TALL

5

Why are there different colors?

What's happening?

The heat from the candle flame melts wax near the base of the wick. Liquefied wax soaks up the unburned part of the wick and into the flame. Heat around the burning part of the wick turns the wax into a gas. This wax vapor mixes with air in the blue part of the flame. The mixture then rises into the middle of the flame, where particles of carbon from the wax glow and give off yellow light.

Sieving solids

Some mixtures can be separated using a sieve. This only works when the mixture contains solids of different sizes. For example, we can sieve soil because it is a mixture of solids such as sand, clay, and humus. The larger particles stay in the sieve, while the smaller ones fall through the holes and collect underneath.

Separating soil

Use two types of sieves to sort soil into four piles of different-sized particles.

YOU WILL NEED
- A COLANDER
- A KITCHEN SIEVE
- FOUR LARGE PIECES OF PAPER
- POTTING SOIL
- A MAGNIFYING GLASS

25

FLASHBACK

Sieving flour

Flour was once made by grinding wheat between two large, revolving stones. About 120 years ago, millers in Hungary and Switzerland began to use cylindrical rollers to powder the grain. Ten sieves with different-sized holes were stacked one above the other. They separated the milled grain into different grades of flour.

3 Gently spread out some of each pile on the sheets. Look carefully through the magnifying glass to compare the sizes of the particles in each of the piles.

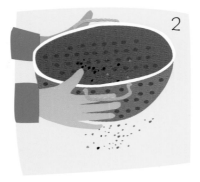

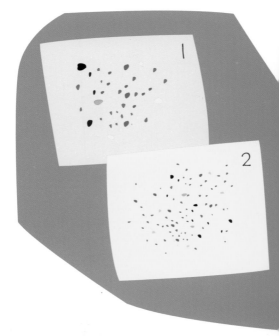

1 Number the sheets of paper 1, 2, 3, and 4. Put some soil into the colander. Hold the colander over sheet 2 and shake gently. When no more soil passes through, pour what's left in the colander onto sheet 1.

2 Take some of the particles from sheet 2 and put them into the kitchen sieve. Tap the sieve over sheet 4 until no more particles pass through. Pour what's left in the sieve onto sheet 3.

Even smaller holes

Put some soil into the cup. Use the rubber band to fasten the foil over the rim of the cup, then prick some tiny holes in the foil with the needle. Turn the cup upside down and gently shake it. Look carefully at the particles that fall onto the paper.

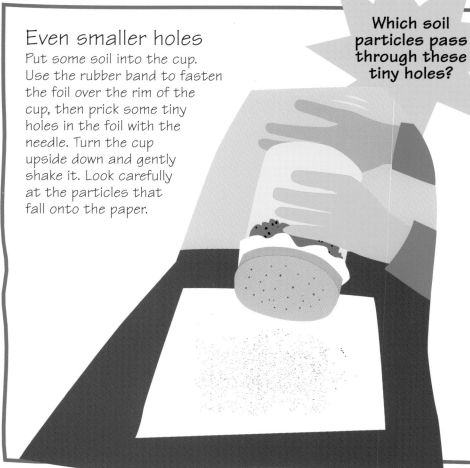

Which soil particles pass through these tiny holes?

YOU WILL NEED

15

◆ WHITE PAPER
◆ A CLEAR PLASTIC CUP
◆ DRY SOIL
◆ ALUMINUM FOIL
◆ A RUBBER BAND
◆ A VERY FINE NEEDLE

What's happening?

The holes in the foil are much less than ⅟₂₅ in. (1mm) across. Clay particles are usually the only part of soil small enough to pass through. These particles appear as a dusty mark on the paper. You would need a powerful microscope to see a single clay particle.

What's happening?

The colander's holes are about ⅛ in. (4mm) across. Only particles that are smaller than these holes pass through the colander. The sieve separates the smaller particles. Its holes are about ⅟₂₅ in. (1mm) across. The particles that stay in the sieve are larger than ⅟₂₅ in. (1mm), but smaller than ⅛ in. (4mm). The ones that go through are smaller than the holes. In this experiment, sheet 1 holds the largest particles, sheet 4 the smallest.

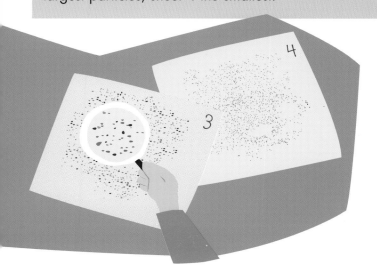

A BREATH OF FRESH AIR

Wood dust from a sanding machine can harm your lungs. These men are wearing safety masks made from paper or cotton fibers. The masks work like a very fine sieve. Gaps between the fibers are large enough to allow air to pass freely, but small enough to stop wood particles from entering the mask.

Solutions and suspensions

Substances like salt and sugar break down, or dissolve, in water. We say that they are soluble. When mixed with water, soluble substances slowly disappear as they dissolve, forming a solution. Substances such as chalk and sand do not dissolve in water. We say that they are insoluble. Shaking an insoluble substance with water scatters the particles through the water and forms a mixture called a suspension.

Solution or suspension?

Add different solids to water and decide which dissolve to form a solution and which scatter to make a suspension.

25

YOU WILL NEED
- FOUR 15-OZ (500-ML) PLASTIC BOTTLES WITH CAPS
- WATER
- A TEASPOON
- A PLASTIC FUNNEL
- SUGAR, FINE SAND, INSTANT COFFEE, AND PLAIN FLOUR

1 Put one spoonful of sugar into one of the bottles using the plastic funnel. Add the sugar slowly so that it does not block the neck of the funnel.

3 Look carefully at each bottle to see if you can still see solid particles. Which solids form solutions? Which solids form suspensions?

2 Repeat step 1 with the other solids, placing each one in its own bottle. Now fill each bottle halfway with water and screw on the cap. Shake each bottle ten times.

What's happening?

Sugar and instant coffee granules dissolve in water to make a solution. All solutions are clear—you can see right through them. A sugar solution is colorless, and a coffee solution is brown. Sand and flour do not dissolve. Shaking them with water creates a suspension. Larger grains quickly settle to the bottom. Suspensions are not clear, and you cannot see through them easily.

Investigating milk

Is milk a solution or a suspension? Find out by adding just one or two drops of milk to a cup of water. Look closely as the milk falls through the water.

YOU WILL NEED
- A TALL, CLEAR PLASTIC CUP OF WATER
- MILK
- A TEASPOON

5

Is milk a single substance or a mixture?

What's happening?
You cannot see clearly through milk, even when you add it to water. Milk consists of droplets of fat suspended in water. Fat is insoluble in water, and the droplets are too small to settle. Scientists call mixtures like milk emulsions. This name is also given to emulsion paint, which consists of microscopic, colored droplets of oil suspended in water.

Creating colors
Paint is colored because it contains tiny, colored particles called pigment. These particles are suspended in a liquid called a binder, which dries hard when exposed to air. Early artists ground up colored minerals or chemicals to make pigments. To bind the color, they used egg white or sticky oils made from boiled tree sap.

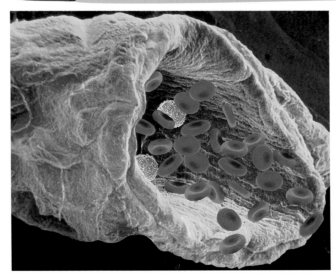

A MIX OF MIXTURES
Blood is both a solution and a suspension. It flows around your body in tubes called blood vessels. Solid red and white blood cells are suspended in a clear liquid called plasma. Plasma is a solution of hundreds of different substances dissolved in water.

Filtering mixtures

Muddy water is an example of a suspension. It consists of tiny, solid particles scattered through a liquid. To separate the particles from the suspension, you can use a filter. Filters work like sieves, but they have microscopic holes called pores and are often made from thick, fluffy paper. The liquid part of a suspension passes through the holes between the paper fibers, while the solid particles are trapped.

Filtering flour

Mixing flour with water makes a cloudy suspension. Coffee filter paper makes the water clear again.

YOU WILL NEED 20
- A COFFEE FILTER FUNNEL
- COFFEE FILTER PAPER
- WATER
- PLAIN FLOUR
- THREE CLEAR PLASTIC CUPS
- A TEASPOON

Which cup has the clearest liquid?

1 Add half a teaspoon of flour to one of the cups. Fill the cup with water and stir the mixture to make a suspension of flour in water.

2 Place the funnel inside an empty cup and put the filter paper inside the funnel. Pour two thirds of the flour-and-water mixture into the filter.

3 When the cup is about a third full, move the funnel and the filter to the last empty cup. Look inside the filter paper when all the liquid has run through. Now look at the liquid in each cup. Can you see a difference?

What's happening?

At first, liquid runs quickly through the filter. Most solid particles are trapped, but some small particles pass through. As a result, the filtered liquid in the first cup is slightly hazy. Liquid then passes slowly as the filter pores get blocked. Now even very small particles cannot pass, so the filtered liquid in the third cup is almost clear.

Filtering through sand

Cut the bottle in half. Place the funneled end facing down into the base of the bottle. Fill the bottle with cotton wool, pebbles, gravel, and sand, as shown, to make your filter. Pour soil mixed with water into the bottle and watch it drip through. What color are the drips? How fast does the water pass through?

YOU WILL NEED
- A 15-OZ. (500-ML) PLASTIC BOTTLE
- SCISSORS
- COTTON WOOL
- SAND, GRAVEL, AND PEBBLES
- POTTING SOIL
- WATER

15

Can sand and rocks make water clean?

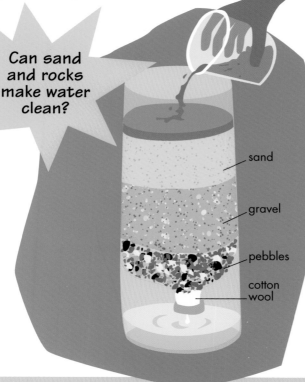

sand

gravel

pebbles

cotton wool

What's happening?

The pebbles, gravel, sand, and the fibers in the cotton wool act together as a filter. They prevent the solids in the water from passing through. The trapped solids are called the residue, and the liquid that passes through is called the filtrate. The tap water we drink often comes from rivers and lakes. It passes through huge sand filters that make the water clear and pure. Added chemicals kill germs.

Filtering germs

Around 1880, doctors discovered that many diseases are caused by germs. They separated germs into two types—filterable and non-filterable. Filterable germs called bacteria cause illnesses such as food poisoning. They are large enough to be trapped by a filter. Non-filterable germs are much smaller and can pass through a filter. They are called viruses, and they cause diseases like chicken pox and flu.

FEEDING THROUGH FILTERS

The humpback whale is a filter feeder. It has hundreds of thin plates called baleen in its mouth. The plates have brushlike fibers that filter food particles from the water. For every 1,040 gallons (4,000l) of water the whale scoops into its mouth, it filters out 45 pounds (20kg) of tiny food particles.

33

Evaporating solutions

You can make a solution by dissolving a solid, such as salt, in water. The solution looks like pure water because the solid has broken down into tiny, invisible particles. Evaporation changes a liquid into a gas, so the amount of liquid slowly decreases. When you evaporate a solution, the solid reappears because there is not enough liquid to dissolve it.

Evaporating salt solution

Solid salt seems to disappear when it dissolves in water. You can evaporate the water to get the solid salt back again.

YOU WILL NEED 20
- SALT
- WARM WATER
- A LARGE PLATE
- A CLEAR PLASTIC CUP
- A TEASPOON

What happens when water evaporates?

1 Pour warm water into the cup until it is one-third full. Add a spoonful of salt and stir until all the salt has dissolved.

2 Pour enough salt solution into the plate to make a shallow pool, then put the plate on a sunny windowsill or in some other warm, dry, airy place.

3 Check the plate twice a day for the next two or three days. What do you see as the water gradually disappears?

What's happening?
Warmth makes water evaporate. Heat energy makes the water particles move fast enough to escape into the air as an invisible gas called water vapor. This means there is less liquid left to dissolve the salt, so the grains of salt reappear. A crusty layer of solid salt is left when all the water has evaporated.

Stalactite on a string

Pour hot water into each jar until it is three-fourths full, then stir in sugar or baking soda until no more will dissolve. Attach a paper clip to each end of the yarn. Drop each end into a jar so that the yarn hangs down between the two jars. Leave in a warm place and inspect the yarn every day for about a week.

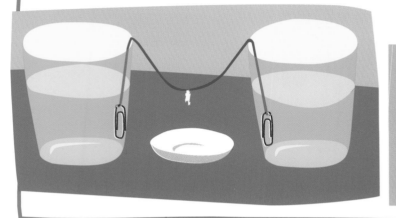

What's happening?

The solution in each jar soaks along the yarn and collects at the lowest point between the jars. Water evaporates from the solution at this point, so that it cannot keep all the solid dissolved. Solid crystals form and grow bigger as the yarn soaks up more solution from the jars.

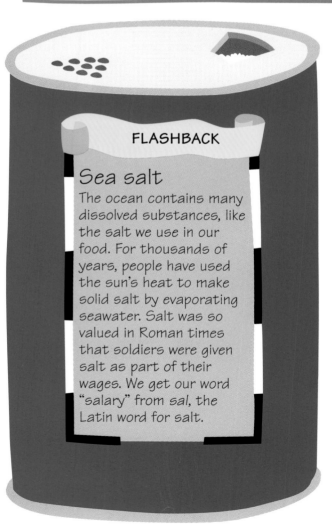

FLASHBACK

Sea salt

The ocean contains many dissolved substances, like the salt we use in our food. For thousands of years, people have used the sun's heat to make solid salt by evaporating seawater. Salt was so valued in Roman times that soldiers were given salt as part of their wages. We get our word "salary" from *sal*, the Latin word for salt.

STALACTITES AND STALAGMITES

Rainwater dissolves limestone rock as it trickles through underground cracks. The water evaporates when it drips from the roof of a cave, leaving a deposit of solid limestone. Stalactites grow down from cave ceilings over thousands of years. Stalagmites grow up from the floor where the drips land.

Saturated solutions

How much sugar can you dissolve in a cup of coffee? The answer is about 20 spoonfuls. If you add any more, solid sugar stays undissolved in the bottom of the cup. When a solution cannot dissolve any more solid, it is called a saturated solution. The amount of solid needed to make a saturated solution varies from one substance to another.

How much solid?

The solubility of a substance is the amount needed to make a saturated solution. Different substances have different solubilities.

Which substance is the most soluble?

1 Label the cups "sugar," "salt," and "baking soda." Fill them halfway with water and place a teaspoon in each.

2 Add a teaspoon of sugar to the cup labeled "sugar." Stir until the solid has dissolved. Now repeat this step in the other cups using baking soda and salt.

3 Add more solid to each cup until no more will dissolve. Count how many spoonfuls of solid dissolve in each cup.

KING ODA

SALT

SUGAR

What's happening?

Each cup contains the same amount of water to make sure the test is fair. More sugar dissolves than salt, so we say that sugar is more soluble than salt. Less baking soda dissolves than either sugar or salt, so it is the least soluble of the three substances.

36

Growing crystals

Fill a cup halfway with warm water. Stir in sugar until no more will dissolve, then pour the clear solution into the other cup, leaving any undissolved sugar behind. Use the pencil and thread to suspend the paper clip in the solution. Look at the paper clip every day for about a week and see what happens.

YOU WILL NEED
◆ SUGAR OR BAKING SODA
◆ TWO CLEAR PLASTIC CUPS
◆ A PENCIL
◆ THREAD
◆ A PAPER CLIP

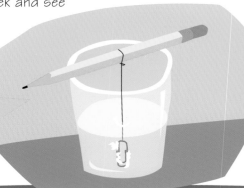

Where do most of the crystals grow?

What's happening?

The water slowly evaporates, and crystals appear when there is not enough water to dissolve of all the solid. Crystals grow on places that aren't smooth, so you will see them first on the edges of the paper clip. The water in the cup disappears slowly because there is only a small surface area from which it can evaporate. This slow evaporation helps large crystals grow.

Fizzing bubbles

Place one bottle of soft drink in the refrigerator and the other in the bucket of warm water. Half an hour later, open both the bottles (over the sink). What do you see?

YOU WILL NEED
◆ TWO SMALL BOTTLES OF SOFT DRINK
◆ A REFRIGERATOR
◆ A BUCKET OF WARM WATER

5

Which drink froths the most?

What's happening?

Soft drinks consist of carbon dioxide gas dissolved in flavored water. You will see more of this gas froth out from the warm drink than from the cold drink. This is because more gas can dissolve in cold liquids than in warm liquids. As you open the bottle, the pressure inside is released, which allows gas to bubble out of the solution and escape.

SUGAR SEEDS
Sugar is made from the juice of sugarcane and sugar beet. Three and a half ounces (100g) of tiny "seed" crystals are added to a huge tank filled with a saturated solution of sugary syrup. In two hours the seeds grow enough to fill the tank with 20 tons of solid sugar crystals.

Glossary

Boil   To heat a liquid until bubbles rise to the surface and burst, releasing vapor. Boiling is the most rapid form of evaporation.

Brittle   Solids that snap easily when bent, or shatter into pieces when struck are brittle. The opposite is durable.

Chemical   Any of the substances that make up materials. Some, called elements, occur naturally and cannot be broken down into other substances. Elements can combine to form other chemicals, such as salt, which is made from the elements sodium and chloride.

Chemist   A scientist who studies how permanent changes can make new substances.

Combustion   Another word for burning.

Compress   To squeeze something so that its volume decreases and it takes up less room. It is fairly easy to compress gases. It is almost impossible to compress liquids or solids.

Condense   To change a gas into a liquid, usually by cooling it.

Conductor   A solid that allows heat and electricity to pass through it easily. Metals like copper and aluminum are good conductors.

Contract   To become smaller. Most solids and all liquids and gases contract when their temperatures decrease.

Dissolve   When a substance disappears as it mixes into a liquid, it dissolves. Salt dissolves in water to make salt solution.

Durable   Solids that do not bend easily and that do not break into pieces when struck are

durable. The opposite is brittle.

Elastic   A solid is elastic if it changes shape when it is squeezed or stretched, then returns to its original shape when the squeezing or stretching stops.

Energy   Energy is the ability to do work. Heat and electricity are two types of energy. Fuels contain energy that is released as heat when they burn.

Evaporate   To change a liquid into a vapor (gas), usually by heating it.

Expand   To become larger. Solids, liquids, and gases expand when they are heated and their temperatures increase.

Filtrate   The liquid part of a suspension that passes through a filter.

Force   A push or a pull. Forces can do work and make things speed up, slow down, or change shape.

Freeze   To change a liquid into a solid, usually by cooling it.

Heat   A form of energy. When heat flows into an object, the object's temperature increases. The temperature decreases when heat flows out of an object.

Insoluble   A substance that does not dissolve in a liquid is insoluble.

Insulator   A substance that does not allow heat and electricity to pass through it easily. Most liquids and gases, and some solids, such as wood and plastic, are insulators.

Mass   The amount of matter in an object.

Matter   Anything that has mass and takes up space.

Material   Different kinds of solids that are used to make things. Steel, paper, cotton, stone, and plastic are all materials.

Melt   To change a solid into a liquid, usually by heating it.

Permanent   A change that cannot be reversed is permanent.

Pressure   A measurement of the amount of force pressing on the surface of an object. Your feet exert pressure on the floor. The pressure of the air inside a balloon keeps the rubber stretched outward.

Property   A quality or trait of an object. For example, one property of water is that it is wet. Another property is that it freezes at 32°F (0°C).

Raw materials   Natural substances that are used to make some products. Raw materials are extracted from the ground (for example, iron ore and crude oil), from seawater (bromine and iodine for use in medicine), and from the air (oxygen and nitrogen).

Saturated solution   A solution that cannot dissolve any more of a solid.

Solidify   To change a liquid into a solid, usually by cooling it.

Solubility   A measurement of how much solid or gas dissolves in a certain amount of liquid.

Soluble   A substance that will dissolve in a liquid is soluble.

Solution   The mixture that results when a substance dissolves in a liquid.

Substance   Any kind of matter. A substance can be a solid, a liquid, or a gas.

Suspension   A mixture made by shaking small, insoluble particles with a liquid.

Temperature   A measurement of how hot something is. On the Fahrenheit temperature scale, water freezes at 32° and boils at 212°.

Temporary   A change that can be reversed is temporary.

Vapor   Another word for gas.

Volume   A measurement of the amount of space taken up by an object. The volume of solids is usually measured in cubic feet or cubic meters; the volume of liquids and gases is measured in gallons or liters.

Weight   The force on an object that results when gravity pulls on its mass. Weight is usually measured in pounds or kilograms.

Index

Photography Credits